FOOD DIARY
&
SYMPTOM LOG

NAME:

PHONE NUMBER:

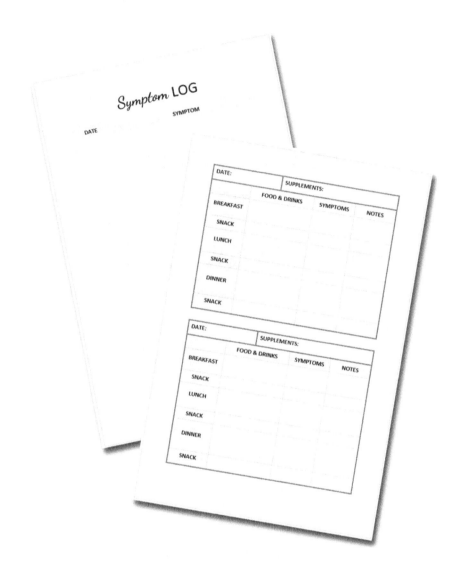

TealBubble Books
www.TealBubble.com

Available from Amazon.com and other online stores.

Symptom LOG

DATE	SYMPTOM

Symptom LOG

DATE	SYMPTOM

Symptom LOG

DATE	SYMPTOM

Symptom LOG

DATE	SYMPTOM

Symptom LOG

DATE	SYMPTOM

Symptom LOG

DATE	SYMPTOM

Symptom LOG

DATE	SYMPTOM

Symptom LOG

DATE	SYMPTOM

DAILY
FOOD
Diary

DATE:	SUPPLEMENTS:		

	FOOD & DRINKS	SYMPTOMS	NOTES
BREAKFAST			
SNACK			
LUNCH			
SNACK			
DINNER			
SNACK			

DATE:	SUPPLEMENTS:		

	FOOD & DRINKS	SYMPTOMS	NOTES
BREAKFAST			
SNACK			
LUNCH			
SNACK			
DINNER			
SNACK			

DATE:	SUPPLEMENTS:		
	FOOD & DRINKS	SYMPTOMS	NOTES
BREAKFAST			
SNACK			
LUNCH			
SNACK			
DINNER			
SNACK			

DATE:	SUPPLEMENTS:		
	FOOD & DRINKS	SYMPTOMS	NOTES
BREAKFAST			
SNACK			
LUNCH			
SNACK			
DINNER			
SNACK			

DATE: 1-12-20	SUPPLEMENTS:		
	FOOD & DRINKS	**SYMPTOMS**	**NOTES**
BREAKFAST	Cheerios apple		
SNACK	chocolate		
LUNCH		Stomach Pain	
SNACK	waffle		
DINNER	Pork potatoes		
SNACK			

DATE:	SUPPLEMENTS:		
	FOOD & DRINKS	**SYMPTOMS**	**NOTES**
BREAKFAST			
SNACK			
LUNCH			
SNACK			
DINNER			
SNACK			

DATE:	SUPPLEMENTS:		
	FOOD & DRINKS	SYMPTOMS	NOTES
BREAKFAST			
SNACK			
LUNCH			
SNACK			
DINNER			
SNACK			

DATE:	SUPPLEMENTS:		
	FOOD & DRINKS	SYMPTOMS	NOTES
BREAKFAST			
SNACK			
LUNCH			
SNACK			
DINNER			
SNACK			

DATE:	SUPPLEMENTS:		
	FOOD & DRINKS	**SYMPTOMS**	**NOTES**
BREAKFAST			
SNACK			
LUNCH			
SNACK			
DINNER			
SNACK			

DATE:	SUPPLEMENTS:		
	FOOD & DRINKS	**SYMPTOMS**	**NOTES**
BREAKFAST			
SNACK			
LUNCH			
SNACK			
DINNER			
SNACK			

DATE:	SUPPLEMENTS:		
	FOOD & DRINKS	**SYMPTOMS**	**NOTES**
BREAKFAST			
SNACK			
LUNCH			
SNACK			
DINNER			
SNACK			

DATE:	SUPPLEMENTS:		
	FOOD & DRINKS	**SYMPTOMS**	**NOTES**
BREAKFAST			
SNACK			
LUNCH			
SNACK			
DINNER			
SNACK			

DATE:	SUPPLEMENTS:		
	FOOD & DRINKS	SYMPTOMS	NOTES
BREAKFAST			
SNACK			
LUNCH			
SNACK			
DINNER			
SNACK			

DATE:	SUPPLEMENTS:		
	FOOD & DRINKS	SYMPTOMS	NOTES
BREAKFAST			
SNACK			
LUNCH			
SNACK			
DINNER			
SNACK			

DATE:	SUPPLEMENTS:		
	FOOD & DRINKS	SYMPTOMS	NOTES
BREAKFAST			
SNACK			
LUNCH			
SNACK			
DINNER			
SNACK			

DATE:	SUPPLEMENTS:		
	FOOD & DRINKS	SYMPTOMS	NOTES
BREAKFAST			
SNACK			
LUNCH			
SNACK			
DINNER			
SNACK			

DATE:	SUPPLEMENTS:		
	FOOD & DRINKS	**SYMPTOMS**	**NOTES**
BREAKFAST			
SNACK			
LUNCH			
SNACK			
DINNER			
SNACK			

DATE:	SUPPLEMENTS:		
	FOOD & DRINKS	**SYMPTOMS**	**NOTES**
BREAKFAST			
SNACK			
LUNCH			
SNACK			
DINNER			
SNACK			

DATE:		SUPPLEMENTS:	
	FOOD & DRINKS	SYMPTOMS	NOTES
BREAKFAST			
SNACK			
LUNCH			
SNACK			
DINNER			
SNACK			

DATE:		SUPPLEMENTS:	
	FOOD & DRINKS	SYMPTOMS	NOTES
BREAKFAST			
SNACK			
LUNCH			
SNACK			
DINNER			
SNACK			

DATE:	SUPPLEMENTS:		
	FOOD & DRINKS	**SYMPTOMS**	**NOTES**
BREAKFAST			
SNACK			
LUNCH			
SNACK			
DINNER			
SNACK			

DATE:	SUPPLEMENTS:		
	FOOD & DRINKS	**SYMPTOMS**	**NOTES**
BREAKFAST			
SNACK			
LUNCH			
SNACK			
DINNER			
SNACK			

DATE:	SUPPLEMENTS:		
	FOOD & DRINKS	SYMPTOMS	NOTES
BREAKFAST			
SNACK			
LUNCH			
SNACK			
DINNER			
SNACK			

DATE:	SUPPLEMENTS:		
	FOOD & DRINKS	SYMPTOMS	NOTES
BREAKFAST			
SNACK			
LUNCH			
SNACK			
DINNER			
SNACK			

DATE:	SUPPLEMENTS:		
	FOOD & DRINKS	SYMPTOMS	NOTES
BREAKFAST			
SNACK			
LUNCH			
SNACK			
DINNER			
SNACK			

DATE:	SUPPLEMENTS:		
	FOOD & DRINKS	SYMPTOMS	NOTES
BREAKFAST			
SNACK			
LUNCH			
SNACK			
DINNER			
SNACK			

DATE:	SUPPLEMENTS:		
	FOOD & DRINKS	SYMPTOMS	NOTES
BREAKFAST			
SNACK			
LUNCH			
SNACK			
DINNER			
SNACK			

DATE:	SUPPLEMENTS:		
	FOOD & DRINKS	SYMPTOMS	NOTES
BREAKFAST			
SNACK			
LUNCH			
SNACK			
DINNER			
SNACK			

DATE:	SUPPLEMENTS:		
	FOOD & DRINKS	SYMPTOMS	NOTES
BREAKFAST			
SNACK			
LUNCH			
SNACK			
DINNER			
SNACK			

DATE:	SUPPLEMENTS:		
	FOOD & DRINKS	SYMPTOMS	NOTES
BREAKFAST			
SNACK			
LUNCH			
SNACK			
DINNER			
SNACK			

DATE:	SUPPLEMENTS:		
	FOOD & DRINKS	SYMPTOMS	NOTES
BREAKFAST			
SNACK			
LUNCH			
SNACK			
DINNER			
SNACK			

DATE:	SUPPLEMENTS:		
	FOOD & DRINKS	SYMPTOMS	NOTES
BREAKFAST			
SNACK			
LUNCH			
SNACK			
DINNER			
SNACK			

DATE:	SUPPLEMENTS:		
	FOOD & DRINKS	SYMPTOMS	NOTES
BREAKFAST			
SNACK			
LUNCH			
SNACK			
DINNER			
SNACK			

DATE:	SUPPLEMENTS:		
	FOOD & DRINKS	SYMPTOMS	NOTES
BREAKFAST			
SNACK			
LUNCH			
SNACK			
DINNER			
SNACK			

DATE:	SUPPLEMENTS:		
	FOOD & DRINKS	SYMPTOMS	NOTES
BREAKFAST			
SNACK			
LUNCH			
SNACK			
DINNER			
SNACK			

DATE:	SUPPLEMENTS:		
	FOOD & DRINKS	SYMPTOMS	NOTES
BREAKFAST			
SNACK			
LUNCH			
SNACK			
DINNER			
SNACK			

DATE:	SUPPLEMENTS:		
	FOOD & DRINKS	SYMPTOMS	NOTES
BREAKFAST			
SNACK			
LUNCH			
SNACK			
DINNER			
SNACK			

DATE:	SUPPLEMENTS:		
	FOOD & DRINKS	SYMPTOMS	NOTES
BREAKFAST			
SNACK			
LUNCH			
SNACK			
DINNER			
SNACK			

DATE:	SUPPLEMENTS:		
	FOOD & DRINKS	**SYMPTOMS**	**NOTES**
BREAKFAST			
SNACK			
LUNCH			
SNACK			
DINNER			
SNACK			

DATE:	SUPPLEMENTS:		
	FOOD & DRINKS	**SYMPTOMS**	**NOTES**
BREAKFAST			
SNACK			
LUNCH			
SNACK			
DINNER			
SNACK			

DATE:	SUPPLEMENTS:		
	FOOD & DRINKS	**SYMPTOMS**	**NOTES**
BREAKFAST			
SNACK			
LUNCH			
SNACK			
DINNER			
SNACK			

DATE:	SUPPLEMENTS:		
	FOOD & DRINKS	**SYMPTOMS**	**NOTES**
BREAKFAST			
SNACK			
LUNCH			
SNACK			
DINNER			
SNACK			

DATE:	SUPPLEMENTS:		
	FOOD & DRINKS	SYMPTOMS	NOTES
BREAKFAST			
SNACK			
LUNCH			
SNACK			
DINNER			
SNACK			

DATE:	SUPPLEMENTS:		
	FOOD & DRINKS	SYMPTOMS	NOTES
BREAKFAST			
SNACK			
LUNCH			
SNACK			
DINNER			
SNACK			

DATE:	SUPPLEMENTS:		
	FOOD & DRINKS	SYMPTOMS	NOTES
BREAKFAST			
SNACK			
LUNCH			
SNACK			
DINNER			
SNACK			

DATE:	SUPPLEMENTS:		
	FOOD & DRINKS	SYMPTOMS	NOTES
BREAKFAST			
SNACK			
LUNCH			
SNACK			
DINNER			
SNACK			

DATE:	SUPPLEMENTS:		
	FOOD & DRINKS	SYMPTOMS	NOTES
BREAKFAST			
SNACK			
LUNCH			
SNACK			
DINNER			
SNACK			

DATE:	SUPPLEMENTS:		
	FOOD & DRINKS	SYMPTOMS	NOTES
BREAKFAST			
SNACK			
LUNCH			
SNACK			
DINNER			
SNACK			

DATE:	SUPPLEMENTS:		
	FOOD & DRINKS	**SYMPTOMS**	**NOTES**
BREAKFAST			
SNACK			
LUNCH			
SNACK			
DINNER			
SNACK			

DATE:	SUPPLEMENTS:		
	FOOD & DRINKS	**SYMPTOMS**	**NOTES**
BREAKFAST			
SNACK			
LUNCH			
SNACK			
DINNER			
SNACK			

DATE:	SUPPLEMENTS:		
	FOOD & DRINKS	SYMPTOMS	NOTES
BREAKFAST			
SNACK			
LUNCH			
SNACK			
DINNER			
SNACK			

DATE:	SUPPLEMENTS:		
	FOOD & DRINKS	SYMPTOMS	NOTES
BREAKFAST			
SNACK			
LUNCH			
SNACK			
DINNER			
SNACK			

DATE:	SUPPLEMENTS:		
	FOOD & DRINKS	SYMPTOMS	NOTES
BREAKFAST			
SNACK			
LUNCH			
SNACK			
DINNER			
SNACK			

DATE:	SUPPLEMENTS:		
	FOOD & DRINKS	SYMPTOMS	NOTES
BREAKFAST			
SNACK			
LUNCH			
SNACK			
DINNER			
SNACK			

DATE:	SUPPLEMENTS:		
	FOOD & DRINKS	**SYMPTOMS**	**NOTES**
BREAKFAST			
SNACK			
LUNCH			
SNACK			
DINNER			
SNACK			

DATE:	SUPPLEMENTS:		
	FOOD & DRINKS	**SYMPTOMS**	**NOTES**
BREAKFAST			
SNACK			
LUNCH			
SNACK			
DINNER			
SNACK			

DATE:	SUPPLEMENTS:		
	FOOD & DRINKS	**SYMPTOMS**	**NOTES**
BREAKFAST			
SNACK			
LUNCH			
SNACK			
DINNER			
SNACK			

DATE:	SUPPLEMENTS:		
	FOOD & DRINKS	**SYMPTOMS**	**NOTES**
BREAKFAST			
SNACK			
LUNCH			
SNACK			
DINNER			
SNACK			

DATE:	SUPPLEMENTS:		
	FOOD & DRINKS	**SYMPTOMS**	**NOTES**
BREAKFAST			
SNACK			
LUNCH			
SNACK			
DINNER			
SNACK			

DATE:	SUPPLEMENTS:		
	FOOD & DRINKS	**SYMPTOMS**	**NOTES**
BREAKFAST			
SNACK			
LUNCH			
SNACK			
DINNER			
SNACK			

DATE:	SUPPLEMENTS:		
	FOOD & DRINKS	**SYMPTOMS**	**NOTES**
BREAKFAST			
SNACK			
LUNCH			
SNACK			
DINNER			
SNACK			

DATE:	SUPPLEMENTS:		
	FOOD & DRINKS	**SYMPTOMS**	**NOTES**
BREAKFAST			
SNACK			
LUNCH			
SNACK			
DINNER			
SNACK			

DATE:	SUPPLEMENTS:		
	FOOD & DRINKS	**SYMPTOMS**	**NOTES**
BREAKFAST			
SNACK			
LUNCH			
SNACK			
DINNER			
SNACK			

DATE:	SUPPLEMENTS:		
	FOOD & DRINKS	**SYMPTOMS**	**NOTES**
BREAKFAST			
SNACK			
LUNCH			
SNACK			
DINNER			
SNACK			

DATE:	SUPPLEMENTS:		
	FOOD & DRINKS	SYMPTOMS	NOTES
BREAKFAST			
SNACK			
LUNCH			
SNACK			
DINNER			
SNACK			

DATE:	SUPPLEMENTS:		
	FOOD & DRINKS	SYMPTOMS	NOTES
BREAKFAST			
SNACK			
LUNCH			
SNACK			
DINNER			
SNACK			

DATE:	SUPPLEMENTS:		
	FOOD & DRINKS	**SYMPTOMS**	**NOTES**
BREAKFAST			
SNACK			
LUNCH			
SNACK			
DINNER			
SNACK			

DATE:	SUPPLEMENTS:		
	FOOD & DRINKS	**SYMPTOMS**	**NOTES**
BREAKFAST			
SNACK			
LUNCH			
SNACK			
DINNER			
SNACK			

DATE:	SUPPLEMENTS:		
	FOOD & DRINKS	**SYMPTOMS**	**NOTES**
BREAKFAST			
SNACK			
LUNCH			
SNACK			
DINNER			
SNACK			

DATE:	SUPPLEMENTS:		
	FOOD & DRINKS	**SYMPTOMS**	**NOTES**
BREAKFAST			
SNACK			
LUNCH			
SNACK			
DINNER			
SNACK			

DATE:	SUPPLEMENTS:		
	FOOD & DRINKS	**SYMPTOMS**	**NOTES**
BREAKFAST			
SNACK			
LUNCH			
SNACK			
DINNER			
SNACK			

DATE:	SUPPLEMENTS:		
	FOOD & DRINKS	**SYMPTOMS**	**NOTES**
BREAKFAST			
SNACK			
LUNCH			
SNACK			
DINNER			
SNACK			

DATE:	SUPPLEMENTS:		
	FOOD & DRINKS	SYMPTOMS	NOTES
BREAKFAST			
SNACK			
LUNCH			
SNACK			
DINNER			
SNACK			

DATE:	SUPPLEMENTS:		
	FOOD & DRINKS	SYMPTOMS	NOTES
BREAKFAST			
SNACK			
LUNCH			
SNACK			
DINNER			
SNACK			

DATE:	SUPPLEMENTS:		
	FOOD & DRINKS	**SYMPTOMS**	**NOTES**
BREAKFAST			
SNACK			
LUNCH			
SNACK			
DINNER			
SNACK			

DATE:	SUPPLEMENTS:		
	FOOD & DRINKS	**SYMPTOMS**	**NOTES**
BREAKFAST			
SNACK			
LUNCH			
SNACK			
DINNER			
SNACK			

DATE:	SUPPLEMENTS:		
	FOOD & DRINKS	**SYMPTOMS**	**NOTES**
BREAKFAST			
SNACK			
LUNCH			
SNACK			
DINNER			
SNACK			

DATE:	SUPPLEMENTS:		
	FOOD & DRINKS	**SYMPTOMS**	**NOTES**
BREAKFAST			
SNACK			
LUNCH			
SNACK			
DINNER			
SNACK			

DATE:	SUPPLEMENTS:		
	FOOD & DRINKS	SYMPTOMS	NOTES
BREAKFAST			
SNACK			
LUNCH			
SNACK			
DINNER			
SNACK			

DATE:	SUPPLEMENTS:		
	FOOD & DRINKS	SYMPTOMS	NOTES
BREAKFAST			
SNACK			
LUNCH			
SNACK			
DINNER			
SNACK			

DATE:	SUPPLEMENTS:		
	FOOD & DRINKS	SYMPTOMS	NOTES
BREAKFAST			
SNACK			
LUNCH			
SNACK			
DINNER			
SNACK			

DATE:	SUPPLEMENTS:		
	FOOD & DRINKS	SYMPTOMS	NOTES
BREAKFAST			
SNACK			
LUNCH			
SNACK			
DINNER			
SNACK			

DATE:	SUPPLEMENTS:		
	FOOD & DRINKS	SYMPTOMS	NOTES
BREAKFAST			
SNACK			
LUNCH			
SNACK			
DINNER			
SNACK			

DATE:	SUPPLEMENTS:		
	FOOD & DRINKS	SYMPTOMS	NOTES
BREAKFAST			
SNACK			
LUNCH			
SNACK			
DINNER			
SNACK			

DATE:		SUPPLEMENTS:		
	FOOD & DRINKS	**SYMPTOMS**	**NOTES**	
BREAKFAST				
SNACK				
LUNCH				
SNACK				
DINNER				
SNACK				

DATE:		SUPPLEMENTS:		
	FOOD & DRINKS	**SYMPTOMS**	**NOTES**	
BREAKFAST				
SNACK				
LUNCH				
SNACK				
DINNER				
SNACK				

DATE:	SUPPLEMENTS:		
	FOOD & DRINKS	SYMPTOMS	NOTES
BREAKFAST			
SNACK			
LUNCH			
SNACK			
DINNER			
SNACK			

DATE:	SUPPLEMENTS:		
	FOOD & DRINKS	SYMPTOMS	NOTES
BREAKFAST			
SNACK			
LUNCH			
SNACK			
DINNER			
SNACK			

DATE:	SUPPLEMENTS:		
	FOOD & DRINKS	**SYMPTOMS**	**NOTES**
BREAKFAST			
SNACK			
LUNCH			
SNACK			
DINNER			
SNACK			

DATE:	SUPPLEMENTS:		
	FOOD & DRINKS	**SYMPTOMS**	**NOTES**
BREAKFAST			
SNACK			
LUNCH			
SNACK			
DINNER			
SNACK			

DATE:	SUPPLEMENTS:		
	FOOD & DRINKS	SYMPTOMS	NOTES
BREAKFAST			
SNACK			
LUNCH			
SNACK			
DINNER			
SNACK			

DATE:	SUPPLEMENTS:		
	FOOD & DRINKS	SYMPTOMS	NOTES
BREAKFAST			
SNACK			
LUNCH			
SNACK			
DINNER			
SNACK			

DATE:	SUPPLEMENTS:		
	FOOD & DRINKS	SYMPTOMS	NOTES
BREAKFAST			
SNACK			
LUNCH			
SNACK			
DINNER			
SNACK			

DATE:	SUPPLEMENTS:		
	FOOD & DRINKS	SYMPTOMS	NOTES
BREAKFAST			
SNACK			
LUNCH			
SNACK			
DINNER			
SNACK			

DATE:	SUPPLEMENTS:		
	FOOD & DRINKS	SYMPTOMS	NOTES
BREAKFAST			
SNACK			
LUNCH			
SNACK			
DINNER			
SNACK			

DATE:	SUPPLEMENTS:		
	FOOD & DRINKS	SYMPTOMS	NOTES
BREAKFAST			
SNACK			
LUNCH			
SNACK			
DINNER			
SNACK			

DATE:	SUPPLEMENTS:		
	FOOD & DRINKS	SYMPTOMS	NOTES
BREAKFAST			
SNACK			
LUNCH			
SNACK			
DINNER			
SNACK			

DATE:	SUPPLEMENTS:		
	FOOD & DRINKS	SYMPTOMS	NOTES
BREAKFAST			
SNACK			
LUNCH			
SNACK			
DINNER			
SNACK			

DATE:	SUPPLEMENTS:		
	FOOD & DRINKS	**SYMPTOMS**	**NOTES**
BREAKFAST			
SNACK			
LUNCH			
SNACK			
DINNER			
SNACK			

DATE:	SUPPLEMENTS:		
	FOOD & DRINKS	**SYMPTOMS**	**NOTES**
BREAKFAST			
SNACK			
LUNCH			
SNACK			
DINNER			
SNACK			

DATE:	SUPPLEMENTS:		
	FOOD & DRINKS	**SYMPTOMS**	**NOTES**
BREAKFAST			
SNACK			
LUNCH			
SNACK			
DINNER			
SNACK			

DATE:	SUPPLEMENTS:		
	FOOD & DRINKS	**SYMPTOMS**	**NOTES**
BREAKFAST			
SNACK			
LUNCH			
SNACK			
DINNER			
SNACK			

DATE:		SUPPLEMENTS:	
	FOOD & DRINKS	**SYMPTOMS**	**NOTES**
BREAKFAST			
SNACK			
LUNCH			
SNACK			
DINNER			
SNACK			

DATE:		SUPPLEMENTS:	
	FOOD & DRINKS	**SYMPTOMS**	**NOTES**
BREAKFAST			
SNACK			
LUNCH			
SNACK			
DINNER			
SNACK			

DATE:	SUPPLEMENTS:		
	FOOD & DRINKS	**SYMPTOMS**	**NOTES**
BREAKFAST			
SNACK			
LUNCH			
SNACK			
DINNER			
SNACK			

DATE:	SUPPLEMENTS:		
	FOOD & DRINKS	**SYMPTOMS**	**NOTES**
BREAKFAST			
SNACK			
LUNCH			
SNACK			
DINNER			
SNACK			

DATE:	SUPPLEMENTS:		
	FOOD & DRINKS	SYMPTOMS	NOTES
BREAKFAST			
SNACK			
LUNCH			
SNACK			
DINNER			
SNACK			

DATE:	SUPPLEMENTS:		
	FOOD & DRINKS	SYMPTOMS	NOTES
BREAKFAST			
SNACK			
LUNCH			
SNACK			
DINNER			
SNACK			

DATE:	SUPPLEMENTS:		
	FOOD & DRINKS	SYMPTOMS	NOTES
BREAKFAST			
SNACK			
LUNCH			
SNACK			
DINNER			
SNACK			

DATE:	SUPPLEMENTS:		
	FOOD & DRINKS	SYMPTOMS	NOTES
BREAKFAST			
SNACK			
LUNCH			
SNACK			
DINNER			
SNACK			

DATE:	SUPPLEMENTS:		
	FOOD & DRINKS	SYMPTOMS	NOTES
BREAKFAST			
SNACK			
LUNCH			
SNACK			
DINNER			
SNACK			

DATE:	SUPPLEMENTS:		
	FOOD & DRINKS	SYMPTOMS	NOTES
BREAKFAST			
SNACK			
LUNCH			
SNACK			
DINNER			
SNACK			

DATE:	SUPPLEMENTS:		
	FOOD & DRINKS	SYMPTOMS	NOTES
BREAKFAST			
SNACK			
LUNCH			
SNACK			
DINNER			
SNACK			

DATE:	SUPPLEMENTS:		
	FOOD & DRINKS	SYMPTOMS	NOTES
BREAKFAST			
SNACK			
LUNCH			
SNACK			
DINNER			
SNACK			

DATE:	SUPPLEMENTS:		
	FOOD & DRINKS	SYMPTOMS	NOTES
BREAKFAST			
SNACK			
LUNCH			
SNACK			
DINNER			
SNACK			

DATE:	SUPPLEMENTS:		
	FOOD & DRINKS	SYMPTOMS	NOTES
BREAKFAST			
SNACK			
LUNCH			
SNACK			
DINNER			
SNACK			

DATE:	SUPPLEMENTS:		
	FOOD & DRINKS	SYMPTOMS	NOTES
BREAKFAST			
SNACK			
LUNCH			
SNACK			
DINNER			
SNACK			

DATE:	SUPPLEMENTS:		
	FOOD & DRINKS	SYMPTOMS	NOTES
BREAKFAST			
SNACK			
LUNCH			
SNACK			
DINNER			
SNACK			

DATE:	SUPPLEMENTS:		
	FOOD & DRINKS	SYMPTOMS	NOTES
BREAKFAST			
SNACK			
LUNCH			
SNACK			
DINNER			
SNACK			

DATE:	SUPPLEMENTS:		
	FOOD & DRINKS	SYMPTOMS	NOTES
BREAKFAST			
SNACK			
LUNCH			
SNACK			
DINNER			
SNACK			

DATE:	SUPPLEMENTS:		
	FOOD & DRINKS	SYMPTOMS	NOTES
BREAKFAST			
SNACK			
LUNCH			
SNACK			
DINNER			
SNACK			

DATE:	SUPPLEMENTS:		
	FOOD & DRINKS	SYMPTOMS	NOTES
BREAKFAST			
SNACK			
LUNCH			
SNACK			
DINNER			
SNACK			

DATE:	SUPPLEMENTS:		
	FOOD & DRINKS	**SYMPTOMS**	**NOTES**
BREAKFAST			
SNACK			
LUNCH			
SNACK			
DINNER			
SNACK			

DATE:	SUPPLEMENTS:		
	FOOD & DRINKS	**SYMPTOMS**	**NOTES**
BREAKFAST			
SNACK			
LUNCH			
SNACK			
DINNER			
SNACK			

DATE:	SUPPLEMENTS:		
	FOOD & DRINKS	SYMPTOMS	NOTES
BREAKFAST			
SNACK			
LUNCH			
SNACK			
DINNER			
SNACK			

DATE:	SUPPLEMENTS:		
	FOOD & DRINKS	SYMPTOMS	NOTES
BREAKFAST			
SNACK			
LUNCH			
SNACK			
DINNER			
SNACK			

DATE:	SUPPLEMENTS:		
	FOOD & DRINKS	SYMPTOMS	NOTES
BREAKFAST			
SNACK			
LUNCH			
SNACK			
DINNER			
SNACK			

DATE:	SUPPLEMENTS:		
	FOOD & DRINKS	SYMPTOMS	NOTES
BREAKFAST			
SNACK			
LUNCH			
SNACK			
DINNER			
SNACK			

DATE:	SUPPLEMENTS:		
	FOOD & DRINKS	SYMPTOMS	NOTES
BREAKFAST			
SNACK			
LUNCH			
SNACK			
DINNER			
SNACK			

DATE:	SUPPLEMENTS:		
	FOOD & DRINKS	SYMPTOMS	NOTES
BREAKFAST			
SNACK			
LUNCH			
SNACK			
DINNER			
SNACK			

DATE:	SUPPLEMENTS:		
	FOOD & DRINKS	SYMPTOMS	NOTES
BREAKFAST			
SNACK			
LUNCH			
SNACK			
DINNER			
SNACK			

DATE:	SUPPLEMENTS:		
	FOOD & DRINKS	SYMPTOMS	NOTES
BREAKFAST			
SNACK			
LUNCH			
SNACK			
DINNER			
SNACK			

DATE:	SUPPLEMENTS:		
	FOOD & DRINKS	SYMPTOMS	NOTES
BREAKFAST			
SNACK			
LUNCH			
SNACK			
DINNER			
SNACK			

DATE:	SUPPLEMENTS:		
	FOOD & DRINKS	SYMPTOMS	NOTES
BREAKFAST			
SNACK			
LUNCH			
SNACK			
DINNER			
SNACK			

DATE:	SUPPLEMENTS:		
	FOOD & DRINKS	**SYMPTOMS**	**NOTES**
BREAKFAST			
SNACK			
LUNCH			
SNACK			
DINNER			
SNACK			

DATE:	SUPPLEMENTS:		
	FOOD & DRINKS	**SYMPTOMS**	**NOTES**
BREAKFAST			
SNACK			
LUNCH			
SNACK			
DINNER			
SNACK			

DATE:	SUPPLEMENTS:		
	FOOD & DRINKS	SYMPTOMS	NOTES
BREAKFAST			
SNACK			
LUNCH			
SNACK			
DINNER			
SNACK			

DATE:	SUPPLEMENTS:		
	FOOD & DRINKS	SYMPTOMS	NOTES
BREAKFAST			
SNACK			
LUNCH			
SNACK			
DINNER			
SNACK			

DATE:	SUPPLEMENTS:		
	FOOD & DRINKS	**SYMPTOMS**	**NOTES**
BREAKFAST			
SNACK			
LUNCH			
SNACK			
DINNER			
SNACK			

DATE:	SUPPLEMENTS:		
	FOOD & DRINKS	**SYMPTOMS**	**NOTES**
BREAKFAST			
SNACK			
LUNCH			
SNACK			
DINNER			
SNACK			

DATE:	SUPPLEMENTS:		
	FOOD & DRINKS	SYMPTOMS	NOTES
BREAKFAST			
SNACK			
LUNCH			
SNACK			
DINNER			
SNACK			

DATE:	SUPPLEMENTS:		
	FOOD & DRINKS	SYMPTOMS	NOTES
BREAKFAST			
SNACK			
LUNCH			
SNACK			
DINNER			
SNACK			

DATE:	SUPPLEMENTS:		
	FOOD & DRINKS	**SYMPTOMS**	**NOTES**
BREAKFAST			
SNACK			
LUNCH			
SNACK			
DINNER			
SNACK			

DATE:	SUPPLEMENTS:		
	FOOD & DRINKS	**SYMPTOMS**	**NOTES**
BREAKFAST			
SNACK			
LUNCH			
SNACK			
DINNER			
SNACK			

DATE:	SUPPLEMENTS:		
	FOOD & DRINKS	SYMPTOMS	NOTES
BREAKFAST			
SNACK			
LUNCH			
SNACK			
DINNER			
SNACK			

DATE:	SUPPLEMENTS:		
	FOOD & DRINKS	SYMPTOMS	NOTES
BREAKFAST			
SNACK			
LUNCH			
SNACK			
DINNER			
SNACK			

DATE:	SUPPLEMENTS:		
	FOOD & DRINKS	**SYMPTOMS**	**NOTES**
BREAKFAST			
SNACK			
LUNCH			
SNACK			
DINNER			
SNACK			

DATE:	SUPPLEMENTS:		
	FOOD & DRINKS	**SYMPTOMS**	**NOTES**
BREAKFAST			
SNACK			
LUNCH			
SNACK			
DINNER			
SNACK			

DATE:	SUPPLEMENTS:		
	FOOD & DRINKS	SYMPTOMS	NOTES
BREAKFAST			
SNACK			
LUNCH			
SNACK			
DINNER			
SNACK			

DATE:	SUPPLEMENTS:		
	FOOD & DRINKS	SYMPTOMS	NOTES
BREAKFAST			
SNACK			
LUNCH			
SNACK			
DINNER			
SNACK			

DATE:		SUPPLEMENTS:	
	FOOD & DRINKS	SYMPTOMS	NOTES
BREAKFAST			
SNACK			
LUNCH			
SNACK			
DINNER			
SNACK			

DATE:		SUPPLEMENTS:	
	FOOD & DRINKS	SYMPTOMS	NOTES
BREAKFAST			
SNACK			
LUNCH			
SNACK			
DINNER			
SNACK			

DATE:	SUPPLEMENTS:		
	FOOD & DRINKS	SYMPTOMS	NOTES
BREAKFAST			
SNACK			
LUNCH			
SNACK			
DINNER			
SNACK			

DATE:	SUPPLEMENTS:		
	FOOD & DRINKS	SYMPTOMS	NOTES
BREAKFAST			
SNACK			
LUNCH			
SNACK			
DINNER			
SNACK			

DATE:	SUPPLEMENTS:		
	FOOD & DRINKS	SYMPTOMS	NOTES
BREAKFAST			
SNACK			
LUNCH			
SNACK			
DINNER			
SNACK			

DATE:	SUPPLEMENTS:		
	FOOD & DRINKS	SYMPTOMS	NOTES
BREAKFAST			
SNACK			
LUNCH			
SNACK			
DINNER			
SNACK			

DATE:	SUPPLEMENTS:		
	FOOD & DRINKS	SYMPTOMS	NOTES
BREAKFAST			
SNACK			
LUNCH			
SNACK			
DINNER			
SNACK			

DATE:	SUPPLEMENTS:		
	FOOD & DRINKS	SYMPTOMS	NOTES
BREAKFAST			
SNACK			
LUNCH			
SNACK			
DINNER			
SNACK			

DATE:	SUPPLEMENTS:		
	FOOD & DRINKS	**SYMPTOMS**	**NOTES**
BREAKFAST			
SNACK			
LUNCH			
SNACK			
DINNER			
SNACK			

DATE:	SUPPLEMENTS:		
	FOOD & DRINKS	**SYMPTOMS**	**NOTES**
BREAKFAST			
SNACK			
LUNCH			
SNACK			
DINNER			
SNACK			

DATE:	SUPPLEMENTS:		
	FOOD & DRINKS	SYMPTOMS	NOTES
BREAKFAST			
SNACK			
LUNCH			
SNACK			
DINNER			
SNACK			

DATE:	SUPPLEMENTS:		
	FOOD & DRINKS	SYMPTOMS	NOTES
BREAKFAST			
SNACK			
LUNCH			
SNACK			
DINNER			
SNACK			

DATE:	SUPPLEMENTS:		
	FOOD & DRINKS	SYMPTOMS	NOTES
BREAKFAST			
SNACK			
LUNCH			
SNACK			
DINNER			
SNACK			

DATE:	SUPPLEMENTS:		
	FOOD & DRINKS	SYMPTOMS	NOTES
BREAKFAST			
SNACK			
LUNCH			
SNACK			
DINNER			
SNACK			

DATE:	SUPPLEMENTS:		
	FOOD & DRINKS	SYMPTOMS	NOTES
BREAKFAST			
SNACK			
LUNCH			
SNACK			
DINNER			
SNACK			

DATE:	SUPPLEMENTS:		
	FOOD & DRINKS	SYMPTOMS	NOTES
BREAKFAST			
SNACK			
LUNCH			
SNACK			
DINNER			
SNACK			

DATE:	SUPPLEMENTS:		
	FOOD & DRINKS	SYMPTOMS	NOTES
BREAKFAST			
SNACK			
LUNCH			
SNACK			
DINNER			
SNACK			

DATE:	SUPPLEMENTS:		
	FOOD & DRINKS	SYMPTOMS	NOTES
BREAKFAST			
SNACK			
LUNCH			
SNACK			
DINNER			
SNACK			

DATE:	SUPPLEMENTS:		
	FOOD & DRINKS	**SYMPTOMS**	**NOTES**
BREAKFAST			
SNACK			
LUNCH			
SNACK			
DINNER			
SNACK			

DATE:	SUPPLEMENTS:		
	FOOD & DRINKS	**SYMPTOMS**	**NOTES**
BREAKFAST			
SNACK			
LUNCH			
SNACK			
DINNER			
SNACK			

DATE:	SUPPLEMENTS:		
	FOOD & DRINKS	SYMPTOMS	NOTES
BREAKFAST			
SNACK			
LUNCH			
SNACK			
DINNER			
SNACK			

DATE:	SUPPLEMENTS:		
	FOOD & DRINKS	SYMPTOMS	NOTES
BREAKFAST			
SNACK			
LUNCH			
SNACK			
DINNER			
SNACK			

DATE:	SUPPLEMENTS:		
	FOOD & DRINKS	SYMPTOMS	NOTES
BREAKFAST			
SNACK			
LUNCH			
SNACK			
DINNER			
SNACK			

DATE:	SUPPLEMENTS:		
	FOOD & DRINKS	SYMPTOMS	NOTES
BREAKFAST			
SNACK			
LUNCH			
SNACK			
DINNER			
SNACK			

DATE:	SUPPLEMENTS:		
	FOOD & DRINKS	SYMPTOMS	NOTES
BREAKFAST			
SNACK			
LUNCH			
SNACK			
DINNER			
SNACK			

DATE:	SUPPLEMENTS:		
	FOOD & DRINKS	SYMPTOMS	NOTES
BREAKFAST			
SNACK			
LUNCH			
SNACK			
DINNER			
SNACK			

DATE:	SUPPLEMENTS:		
	FOOD & DRINKS	SYMPTOMS	NOTES
BREAKFAST			
SNACK			
LUNCH			
SNACK			
DINNER			
SNACK			

DATE:	SUPPLEMENTS:		
	FOOD & DRINKS	SYMPTOMS	NOTES
BREAKFAST			
SNACK			
LUNCH			
SNACK			
DINNER			
SNACK			

DATE:	SUPPLEMENTS:		
	FOOD & DRINKS	**SYMPTOMS**	**NOTES**
BREAKFAST			
SNACK			
LUNCH			
SNACK			
DINNER			
SNACK			

DATE:	SUPPLEMENTS:		
	FOOD & DRINKS	**SYMPTOMS**	**NOTES**
BREAKFAST			
SNACK			
LUNCH			
SNACK			
DINNER			
SNACK			

DATE:	SUPPLEMENTS:		
	FOOD & DRINKS	SYMPTOMS	NOTES
BREAKFAST			
SNACK			
LUNCH			
SNACK			
DINNER			
SNACK			

DATE:	SUPPLEMENTS:		
	FOOD & DRINKS	SYMPTOMS	NOTES
BREAKFAST			
SNACK			
LUNCH			
SNACK			
DINNER			
SNACK			

DATE:	SUPPLEMENTS:		
	FOOD & DRINKS	SYMPTOMS	NOTES
BREAKFAST			
SNACK			
LUNCH			
SNACK			
DINNER			
SNACK			

DATE:	SUPPLEMENTS:		
	FOOD & DRINKS	SYMPTOMS	NOTES
BREAKFAST			
SNACK			
LUNCH			
SNACK			
DINNER			
SNACK			

DATE:	SUPPLEMENTS:		
	FOOD & DRINKS	**SYMPTOMS**	**NOTES**
BREAKFAST			
SNACK			
LUNCH			
SNACK			
DINNER			
SNACK			

DATE:	SUPPLEMENTS:		
	FOOD & DRINKS	**SYMPTOMS**	**NOTES**
BREAKFAST			
SNACK			
LUNCH			
SNACK			
DINNER			
SNACK			

DATE:	SUPPLEMENTS:		
	FOOD & DRINKS	SYMPTOMS	NOTES
BREAKFAST			
SNACK			
LUNCH			
SNACK			
DINNER			
SNACK			

DATE:	SUPPLEMENTS:		
	FOOD & DRINKS	SYMPTOMS	NOTES
BREAKFAST			
SNACK			
LUNCH			
SNACK			
DINNER			
SNACK			

DATE:	SUPPLEMENTS:		
	FOOD & DRINKS	SYMPTOMS	NOTES
BREAKFAST			
SNACK			
LUNCH			
SNACK			
DINNER			
SNACK			

DATE:	SUPPLEMENTS:		
	FOOD & DRINKS	SYMPTOMS	NOTES
BREAKFAST			
SNACK			
LUNCH			
SNACK			
DINNER			
SNACK			

DATE:	SUPPLEMENTS:		
	FOOD & DRINKS	**SYMPTOMS**	**NOTES**
BREAKFAST			
SNACK			
LUNCH			
SNACK			
DINNER			
SNACK			

DATE:	SUPPLEMENTS:		
	FOOD & DRINKS	**SYMPTOMS**	**NOTES**
BREAKFAST			
SNACK			
LUNCH			
SNACK			
DINNER			
SNACK			

Notes

Notes

Notes

Notes

TealBubble Books
www.TealBubble.com

Available from Amazon.com and other online stores.

Made in the USA
Middletown, DE
01 January 2020

82362094R00066